of thirty-five you will be nostalgic for at the age of forty-five. ★ Write everything down. ★ Keep a journal. ★ Take more pictures. ★ The empty nest is underrated. ★ You can order more than one dessert. ★ You can't own too many black turtleneck sweaters. ★ If the shoe doesn't fit in the shoe store, it's never going to fit. ★ Back up your files. ★ Overinsure everything. ★ There's no point in making piecrust from scratch. ★ The reason you're waking up in the middle of the night is the second glass of wine. ★ The minute you decide to get divorced, go see a lawyer and file the papers. ★ Overtip. ★ Never let them know. ★ There are no secrets.

Someday this will be a funny story

BY NORA EPHRON

FICTION
Heartburn

ESSAYS
I Remember Nothing
I Feel Bad About My Neck
Nora Ephron Collected
Scribble Scribble
Crazy Salad
Wallflower at the Orgy

DRAMA
Lucky Guy
Love, Loss, and What I Wore (with Delia Ephron)
Imaginary Friends

SCREENPLAYS
Julie & Julia
Bewitched (with Delia Ephron)
Hanging Up (with Delia Ephron)
You've Got Mail (with Delia Ephron)
Michael (with Jim Quinlan, Pete Dexter, and Delia Ephron)
Mixed Nuts (with Delia Ephron)
Sleepless in Seattle (with David S. Ward and Jeff Arch)
This Is My Life (with Delia Ephron)
My Blue Heaven
When Harry Met Sally . . .
Cookie (with Alice Arlen)
Heartburn
Silkwood (with Alice Arlen)

The Quotable
NORA EPHRON

Someday this will be a funny story

doubleday

TRANSWORLD PUBLISHERS

UK | USA | Canada | Ireland | Australia
India | New Zealand | South Africa

Transworld is part of the Penguin Random House group of companies
whose addresses can be found at global.penguinrandomhouse.com.

Penguin Random House UK, One Embassy Gardens,
8 Viaduct Gardens, London SW11 7BW

penguin.co.uk

First published in Great Britain in 2026 by Doubleday
an imprint of Transworld Publishers

001

Copyright © 2026 by the Marital Trust f/b/o Nicholas Pileggi

The moral right of the author has been asserted.

Every effort has been made to obtain the necessary permissions with
reference to copyright material, both illustrative and quoted. We apologize
for any omissions in this respect and will be pleased to make the
appropriate acknowledgements in any future edition.

Penguin Random House values and supports copyright. Copyright fuels creativity, encourages diverse voices, promotes freedom of expression and supports a vibrant culture. Thank you for purchasing an authorized edition of this book and for respecting intellectual property laws by not reproducing, scanning or distributing any part of it by any means without permission. You are supporting authors and enabling Penguin Random House to continue to publish books for everyone. No part of this book may be used or reproduced in any manner for the purpose of training artificial intelligence technologies or systems. In accordance with Article 4(3) of the DSM Directive 2019/790, Penguin Random House expressly reserves this work from the text and data mining exception.

Illustrations and chapter head lettering by Heather Gatley
Designed and typeset by Couper Street Type Co.
Printed and bound in Great Britain by Clays Ltd, Elcograf S.p.A.

The authorized representative in the EEA is Penguin Random House Ireland,
Morrison Chambers, 32 Nassau Street, Dublin D02 YH68

A CIP catalogue record for this book is available from the British Library.

ISBN: 9781529980431

Someday this will be a funny story

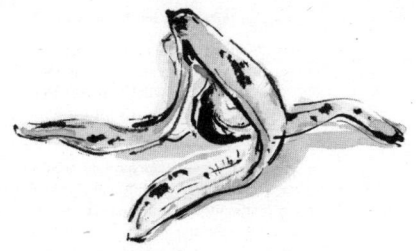

Reading and writing

FREEDOM OF THE PRESS
BELONGS TO THE MAN
WHO OWNS ONE.

I now believe that what my mother meant when she said "Everything is copy" is this: When you slip on a banana peel, people laugh at you; but when you tell people you slipped on a banana peel, it's your laugh.

For many years I was in love with journalism.
I loved smoking and drinking scotch and playing
dollar poker. I didn't know much about anything,
and I was in a profession where you didn't have to.
I loved the speed. I loved the deadlines. You can't
make this stuff up, I used to say.

I think you often have that sense when you write—
that if you can spot something in yourself and
set it down on paper, you're free of it.
And you're not, of course; you've just managed
to set it down on paper, that's all.

The other advantage to all those years in the newspaper business is that I learned to write short. Much too short probably, but as vices go, that's far better than too long.

Reading is everything. Reading makes me feel I've accomplished something, learned something, become a better person. Reading makes me smarter. Reading gives me something to talk about later on. Reading is the unbelievably healthy way my attention deficit disorder medicates itself. Reading is escape and the opposite of escape; it's a way to make contact with reality after a day of making things up, and it's a way of making contact with someone else's imagination that's all too real. Reading is grist. Reading is bliss.

Whenever I read a book I love, I start to remember all the other books that have sent me into rapture, and I can remember where I was living and the couch I was sitting on when I read them.

There's something called the rapture of the deep, and it refers to what happens when a deep-sea diver spends too much time at the bottom of the ocean and can't tell which way is up. When he surfaces, he's liable to have a condition called the bends, where the body can't adapt to the oxygen levels in the atmosphere. All of this happens to me when I surface from a great book.

ALMOST ALL BOOKS THAT
ARE PUBLISHED AS MEMOIRS WERE
INITIALLY WRITTEN AS NOVELS,
AND THEN THE AGENT/EDITOR SAID,
THIS MIGHT WORK BETTER
AS A MEMOIR.

Journalists *are* interesting. They just aren't as interesting as the things they cover.

It's possible to lose sight of this.

I would like not to.

Parents and children

You always think that a bolt of lightning is going to strike and your parents will magically change into the people you wish they were, or back into the people they used to be. But they're never going to. And even though you know they're never going to, you still hope they will.

If you find yourself nostalgic for the ongoing, day-to-day activities required of the modern parent, there's a solution: get a dog. I don't recommend it, because dogs require tremendous commitment, but they definitely give you something to do. Plus, they're very loveable and more important, uncritical. And they can be trained.

Every so often, your children come to visit. They are, amazingly, completely charming people. You can't believe you're lucky enough to know them. They make you laugh. They make you proud. You love them madly. They survived you. You survived them. It crosses your mind that on some level, you spent hours and days and months without laying a glove on them, but don't dwell. There's no point. It's over. Except for the worrying. The worrying is forever.

Many years ago, when I was in analysis, my therapist used to say, "Love is homesickness." What she meant was that you tend to fall in love with someone who reminds you of one of your parents. This, of course, is one of those things analysts say even though it really isn't true. Just about anyone on the planet is capable of reminding you of something about one of your parents, even if it's only a dimple. But I don't mean to digress. The point I want to make is that love may or may not be homesickness, but homesickness is most definitely love.

Meanwhile, you have an extra room. Your child's room. Do not under any circumstances leave your child's room as is. Your child's room is not a shrine. It's not going to the Smithsonian. Turn it into a den, a gym, a guest room, or (if you already have all three) a room for wrapping Christmas presents. Do this as soon as possible. Leaving your child's room as is may encourage your child to return. You do not want this.

Even in the old days, my mother was a washout at hard-core mothering; what she was good at were clever remarks that made you feel immensely adult and, if you thought about it at all, foolish for having wanted anything so mundane as some actual nurturing. Had I been able to talk to her at this moment of crisis, she would probably have said something fabulously brittle like "Take notes."

If pregnancy were a book, they would cut the last two chapters. The beginning is glorious, especially if you're lucky enough not to have morning sickness and if, like me, you've had small breasts all your life.

TRY FLYING ON ANY PLANE WITH A BABY IF YOU WANT A SENSE OF WHAT IT MUST HAVE BEEN LIKE TO BE A LEPER IN THE FOURTEENTH CENTURY.

Marriage and divorce

YOU CAN NEVER KNOW THE TRUTH
OF ANYONE'S MARRIAGE,
INCLUDING YOUR OWN.

The main problem with our marriages was not that our husbands wouldn't share the housework but that we were unbelievably irritable young women and our husbands irritated us unbelievably.

Infidelity doesn't work. You have only a certain amount of energy, and when you spread it around, everything gets confused, and the first thing you know, you can't remember which one you've told which story to.

One thing I have never understood is how to work it so that when you're married, things keep happening to you. Things happen to you when you're single. You meet new men, you travel alone, you learn new tricks, you read Trollope, you try sushi, you buy nightgowns, you shave your legs. Then you get married, and the hair grows in.

It's like a beautiful thing that suddenly turns out to be broken into hundreds of pieces, and even when you glue it back together it's always going to have been horribly broken. That's what marriage is. Pieces break off, and you glue them back on.

YOU ENTER INTO A CERTAIN AMOUNT
OF MADNESS WHEN YOU MARRY
A PERSON WITH PETS.

"You picked the one person on earth you shouldn't be involved with." There's nothing brilliant about that—that's life. Every time you turn around you get involved with the one person on earth you shouldn't get involved with.

It seemed to me that the desire to get married—which, I regret to say, I believe is fundamental and primal in women—is followed almost immediately by an equally fundamental and primal urge, which is to be single.

My marriage to him was as willful an act as
I have ever committed; I married him against all
evidence. I married him believing that marriage
doesn't work, that love dies, that passion fades,
and in so doing I became the kind of romantic
only a cynic is truly capable of being.

It's hard when you don't like someone a friend marries. First of all, it means you pretty much have to confine your friendship to lunch, and I hate lunch. Second of all, it means that even a simple flat inquiry like "How's Helen?" is taken amiss, since your friend always thinks that what you hope he's going to say is "Dead."

Some years ago, the man I am married to told
me he had always had a mad desire to go to an orgy.
Why on earth, I asked. Why not, he said. Because,
I replied, it would be just like the dances at the
YMCA I went to in the seventh grade—
only instead of people walking past me and
rejecting me, they would be stepping over my
naked body and rejecting me.

One good thing I'd like to say about divorce is that it sometimes makes it possible for you to be a much better wife to your next husband because you have a place to direct your anger; it's not directed at the person you're currently with. Another good thing about divorce is that it makes clear something that marriage obscures, which is that you're on your own.

The best divorce is the kind where there are no children. That was my first divorce. You walk out the door and you never look back. There were cats, cats I was wildly attached to; my husband and I spoke in cat voices. Once the marriage was over, I never thought about the cats again.

Once you find out he's cheated on you,
you have to keep finding it out over and over again,
until you've degraded yourself so completely that
there's nothing left to do but walk out.

"I THINK WE'D BETTER HAVE A TALK"
ARE THE SEVEN WORST WORDS IN
THE ENGLISH LANGUAGE.

Sometimes I believe that sex plus guilt equals love, and sometimes I believe that sex plus guilt equals good sex. Sometimes I believe that some people are better at love than others, and sometimes I believe that everyone is faking it. Sometimes I believe that love is essential, and sometimes I believe that the only reason love is essential is that otherwise you spend all your time looking for it.

That's the catch about betrayal, of course: that it feels good, that there's something immensely pleasurable about moving from a complicated relationship which involves minor atrocities on both sides to a nice, neat, simple one where one person has done something so horrible and unforgivable that the other person is immediately absolved of all the low-grade sins of sloth, envy, gluttony, avarice, and I forget the other three.

IT'S MUCH EASIER TO GET OVER SOMEONE IF YOU CAN DELUDE YOURSELF INTO THINKING YOU NEVER REALLY CARED THAT MUCH.

And then the dream breaks into a million tiny pieces. The dream dies. Which leaves you with a choice: you can settle for reality, or you can go off, like a fool, and dream another dream.

I'd known since I was a child that I was going to live in New York City eventually, and that everything in between would just be an intermission. I'd spent all those years imagining what New York was going to be like. I thought it was going to be the most exciting, magical, fraught-with-possibility place that you could ever live; a place where if you really wanted something you might be able to get it; a place where I'd be surrounded by people I was dying to know; a place where I might be able to become the only thing worth being, a journalist. And I'd turned out to be right.

I had never planned to live on the Upper West Side,
but after a few weeks, I couldn't imagine living
anywhere else, and I began, in my manner,
to make a religion out of my neighborhood.
This was probably a consequence of my not having
any other religion in my life, but never mind.

JUST BEFORE I'D MOVED TO NEW YORK, TWO HISTORIC EVENTS OCCURRED: THE BIRTH CONTROL PILL HAD BEEN INVENTED, AND THE FIRST JULIA CHILD COOKBOOK WAS PUBLISHED. AS A RESULT, EVERYONE WAS HAVING SEX, AND WHEN THE SEX WAS OVER, YOU COOKED SOMETHING.

Even the vegetables in New York are better.

It's not just the vegetables, of course. I look out the window and I see the lights and the skyline and the people on the street rushing around looking for action, love, and the world's greatest chocolate chip cookie, and my heart does a little dance.

When my marriage came to an end, I realized that I would never again have to worry about whether the marginal neighborhood where we lived was ever going to have a cheese store. I would be free to move back to New York City—which was not just the Big Apple but Cheese Central.

It's not a purse exactly; it's a bag. It's definitely the best bag I've ever owned. On it is the image of a New York City MetroCard—it's yellow (taxicab yellow, to be exact) and blue (the most horrible blue of all, royal blue)—so it matches nothing at all and therefore, on a deep level, matches everything.

It's made of plastic and is therefore completely waterproof. It's equally unattractive in all seasons of the year. It cost next to nothing (twenty-six dollars), and I will never have to replace it because it seems to be completely indestructible. What's more, never having been in style, it can never go out of style.

The realization that I may have only a few good years remaining has hit me with real force, and I have done a lot of thinking as a result. I would like to come up with something profound, but I haven't. I try to figure out what I really want to do every day, I try to say to myself, If this is one of the last days of my life, am I doing exactly what I want to be doing? I aim low. My idea of a perfect day is a frozen custard at Shake Shack and a walk in the park. (Followed by a Lactaid.) My idea of a perfect night is a good play and dinner at Orso. (But no garlic, or I won't be able to sleep.) The other day I found a bakery that bakes my favorite childhood cake, and it was everything I remembered; it made my week. The other night we were coming up the FDR Drive and Manhattan was doing its fabulous, magical, twinkling thing, and all I could think was how lucky I've been to spend my adult life in New York City.

Food

I have friends who eat egg-white omelettes. Every time I'm forced to watch them eat egg-white omelettes, I feel bad for them. In the first place, egg-white omelettes are tasteless. In the second place, the people who eat them think they are doing something virtuous when they are instead merely misinformed.

I'VE HAD EXACTLY ONE BITE OF MY MAIN COURSE, WHICH IS JUST ENOUGH FOR ME TO REMEMBER THAT, AS USUAL, THE MAIN COURSE ALWAYS DISAPPOINTS. I'M BEGINNING TO WONDER WHETHER THIS IS A METAPHOR, AND IF SO, WHETHER IT'S WORTH DWELLING ON.

Here's the thing about dessert—you want it to last. You want to savor it. Dessert is so delicious. It's so sweet. It's so bad for you so much of the time. And, as with all bad things, you want it to last as long as possible.

I have friends who begin with pasta, and friends who begin with rice, but whenever I fall in love, I begin with potatoes. Sometimes meat and potatoes and sometimes fish and potatoes, but always potatoes. I have made a lot of mistakes falling in love, and regretted most of them, but never the potatoes that went with them.

What I love about cooking is that after a hard day, there is something comforting about the fact that if you melt butter and add flour and then hot stock, *it will get thick!* It's a sure thing! It's a sure thing in a world where nothing is sure; it has a mathematical certainty in a world where those of us who long for some kind of certainty are forced to settle for crossword puzzles.

NOTHING LIKE MASHED POTATOES
WHEN YOU'RE FEELING BLUE.

The other day I felt a cold coming on. So I decided to have chicken soup to ward off the cold. Nevertheless, I got the cold. This happens all the time: you think you're getting a cold; you have chicken soup; you get the cold anyway. So is it possible that chicken soup gives you a cold?

Tasting it again was like being able to turn back the clock, like having the consequences of a mistake erased; it was better than getting a blouse back that the dry cleaners had lost, or a cell phone returned that had been left in the taxi; it was validation of never-giving-up and of hope-springing-eternal; it was many things, it was all things, it was nothing at all; but mostly, it was cabbage strudel.

Style, beauty and getting older

YOU LOSE CLOSE FRIENDS AND DISCOVER ONE OF THE WORST TRUTHS OF OLD AGE: THEY'RE IRREPLACEABLE.

In fact, looking back, it seems to me
that I was clueless until
I was about fifty years old.

The neck is a dead giveaway. Our faces are lies and our necks are the truth. You have to cut open a redwood tree to see how old it is, but you wouldn't have to if it had a neck.

Oh, how I regret not having worn a bikini for the entire year I was twenty-six. If anyone young is reading this, go, right this minute, put on a bikini, and don't take it off until you're thirty-four.

Everybody dies. There's nothing you can do about it. Whether or not you eat six almonds a day. Whether or not you believe in God. (Although there's no question a belief in God would come in handy. It would be great to think there's a plan, and that everything happens for a reason. I don't happen to believe that. And every time one of my friends says to me, "Everything happens for a reason," I would like to smack her.)

I feel bad about my neck. Truly I do. If you saw my neck, you might feel bad about it too, but you'd probably be too polite to let on. If I said something to you on the subject—something like "I absolutely cannot stand my neck"—you'd undoubtedly respond by saying something nice, like "I don't know what you're talking about."

You'd be lying, of course, but I forgive you.

MY EXPERIENCE IS THAT "I DON'T KNOW WHAT YOU'RE TALKING ABOUT" IS CODE FOR "I SEE WHAT YOU MEAN, BUT IF YOU THINK YOU'RE GOING TO TRAP ME INTO ENGAGING ON THIS SUBJECT, YOU'RE CRAZY."

Every so often I read a book about age,
and whoever's writing it says it's great to be old.
It's great to be wise and sage and mellow;
it's great to be at a point where you understand
just what matters in life. I can't stand people
who say things like this.

One of the few advantages to not being beautiful is that one usually gets better-looking as one gets older; I am, in fact, at this very moment gaining my looks.

Here's what happens with a purse. You start small.
You start pledging yourself to neatness. You start
vowing that This Time It Will Be Different.
You start with the things that you absolutely need—
your wallet and a few cosmetics that you actually
put into a brand-new shiny cosmetic bag, the kind
used by your friends who are competent enough
to manage more than one purse at a time.
But within seconds, your purse has accumulated
the debris of a lifetime.

~~~~~

BLACK MAKES YOUR LIFE SO MUCH
SIMPLER. EVERYTHING MATCHES BLACK,
ESPECIALLY BLACK.

~~~~~

The best thing about a pedicure is that most of the year, from September to May to be exact, no one but your loved one knows if you have had one.

I may not be good at purses, but I know that any purse that hangs stiffly on your arm (instead of on your shoulder) adds ten years to your age, and furthermore immobilizes half your body. In a modern world, your arms have to be free. If one of your hands is stuck carrying your purse, it means it's not free for all sorts of exciting things you could be using it for, like shoving your way through crowds, throwing your arms around loved ones, climbing the greasy pole to success, and waving madly for taxis.

You know what maintenance is, I'm sure.
Maintenance is what they mean when they say,
"After a certain point, it's just patch patch patch."

Maintenance is what you have to do just so you can walk out the door knowing that if you go to the market and bump into a guy that rejected you, you won't have to hide behind a stack of canned food. I don't mean to be too literal about this. There are a couple of old boyfriends whom I always worry about bumping into, but there's no chance—if I ever did— that I would recognize either of them. On top of which they live in other cities. But the point is that I still think about them every time I'm tempted to leave the house without eyeliner.

SOMETIMES I THINK THAT NOT HAVING TO WORRY ABOUT YOUR HAIR ANYMORE IS THE SECRET UPSIDE OF DEATH.

Twice a week, I go to a beauty salon and have my hair blown dry. It's cheaper by far than psychoanalysis and much more uplifting.

There's a reason why forty, fifty, and sixty don't look the way they used to, and it's not because of feminism, or better living through exercise. It's because of hair dye.

I would like to be in shape. I would. But every time I try to get into shape, something goes wrong and makes it impossible. Let me make this clear: Every time I get into shape, something breaks.

Death is a sniper. It strikes people you love,
people you like, people you know, it's everywhere.
You could be next. But then you turn out not to be.
But then again you could be.

How to live, love, and, when necessary, get over it

Failure, they say, is a growth experience;
you learn from the failure. I wish that were true.
It seems to me the main thing you learn from
a failure is that it's entirely possible you
will have another failure.

~~~~~~

MY RELIGION IS

GET OVER IT.

~~~~~~

I can make a case that I regret nothing. After all, most of my mistakes turned out to be things I survived, or turned into funny stories, or, on occasion, even made money from.

What failure of imagination had caused me
to forget that life was full of other possibilities,
including the possibility that eventually
I would fall in love again?

I ALMOST FELT SORRY FOR MYSELF.

BUT IT WAS TIME FOR LUNCH.

Because if I tell the story, I control the version. Because if I tell the story, I can make you laugh, and I would rather have you laugh at me than feel sorry for me. Because if I tell the story, it doesn't hurt as much. Because if I tell the story, I can get on with it.

I know that the pendulum often has to swing
a few degrees in the wrong direction before righting
itself, but it does get wearing sometimes waiting
for the center to catch hold.

Here are some questions I am constantly noodling over: Do you splurge or do you hoard? Do you live every day as if it's your last, or do you save your money on the chance you'll live twenty more years? Is life too short, or is it going to be too long? Do you work as hard as you can, or do you slow down to smell the roses? And where do carbohydrates fit into all this? Are we really all going to spend our last years avoiding bread, especially now that bread in America is so unbelievably delicious? And what about chocolate?

Don't underestimate how much antagonism there is toward women and how many people wish we could turn the clock back. One of the things people always say to you if you get upset is "Don't take it personally," but listen hard to what's going on, and please, I beg you, take it personally.

BE THE HEROINE OF YOUR LIFE,
NOT THE VICTIM.

What are you going to do? Everything, is my guess. It will be a little messy, but embrace the mess. It will be complicated, but rejoice in the complications. It will not be anything like what you think it will be like, but surprises are good for you. And don't be frightened: you can always change your mind. I should know: I've had four careers and three husbands.

I care that there's a war in Indochina, and I demonstrate against it; and I care that there's a women's liberation movement, and I demonstrate for it. But I also go to the movies incessantly and have my hair done once a week, and cook dinner every night, and spend hours in front of the mirror trying to make my eyes look symmetrical, and I care about those things, too.

YOUR EDUCATION IS A
DRESS REHEARSAL FOR A LIFE
THAT IS YOURS TO LEAD.

We were indoctrinated in my mother's rules: Never buy a red coat. Red meat keeps your hair from turning gray. You *can* leave the table but you *may not* leave the table. The means and the ends are the same.

That's the truest sign of insanity—
insane people are always sure they're just fine.
It's only the sane people who are willing
to admit they're crazy.

I don't pretend to be able to provide an answer as to why these women put up with what they do, but some of it has to do with a society structured in such a way as to make women believe that to be with a man—any man, on whatever terms— is better than being alone.

I wanted more than anything to be something
I will never be—feminine, and feminine in the
worst way. Submissive. Dependent. Soft-spoken.
Coquettish. I was no good at all at any of it,
no good at being a girl; on the other hand,
I am not half-bad at being a woman.

Whatever you choose, however many roads you travel, I hope that you choose not to be a lady. I hope you will find some way to break the rules and make a little trouble out there. And I also hope you will choose to make some of that trouble on behalf of women.

A NOTE ON SOURCES

The quotations in this book, listed by the pages on which they appear, are taken from the following sources.

Pages 5, 7, 13, 19, 31, 32, 42, 43, 44, 53, 59, 63, 64, 65, 69, 75, 76, 79, 99, 100: *I Remember Nothing*.

Pages 6, 10, 11, 12, 20, 21, 22, 23, 48, 54, 55, 57, 58, 70, 77, 78, 80, 81, 82, 84, 85, 86, 87, 88, 89, 90, 91, 92, 93, 94, 101, 102, 103: *I Feel Bad About My Neck*.

Pages 8, 24, 25, 26, 33, 34, 35, 36, 37, 38, 39, 40, 45, 46, 47, 49, 56, 66, 67, 68, 104, 113: *Heartburn*.

Pages 9, 41, 110: *Wallflower at the Orgy*.

Pages 14, 83, 105, 114: *Crazy Salad and Scribble Scribble*.

Pages 106, 107, 108, 109, 111, 112, 115, 116: *The Most of Nora Ephron*.

A NOTE ABOUT THE AUTHOR

NORA EPHRON was the author of the bestsellers *I Feel Bad About My Neck*, *I Remember Nothing*, and *Heartburn*. She received Academy Award nominations for Best Original Screenplay for *When Harry Met Sally . . .* , *Silkwood*, and *Sleepless in Seattle*, which she also directed. Her other credits include the plays *Imaginary Friends; Love, Loss, and What I Wore;* and *Lucky Guy;* and the films *You've Got Mail* and *Julie & Julia*, both of which she wrote and directed.